FELT

SEW

GOOD

30 SIMPLE &
STYLISH FELT
PROJECTS

FELT SEW GOOD

30 SIMPLE & STYLISH FELT PROJECTS

Christine Leech

BARRON'S

Photography by Keiko Oikawa

FOR JO, MY BRILLIANT SISTER

4

WHAT'S INSIDE?

CONTENTS

INTRODUCTION

When I started telling people I was working on a craft book about felt, almost everyone replied, "Ooh, like Fuzzy Felt?" Well actually, no, not really. Though I loved playing with the simple felt shapes when I was younger, I wanted this book to showcase the versatility of felt, from sophisticated Scandinavian inspired homewares, such as the Scallop Pillow (see page 106) and the Hanging Bluebirds (see page 76), to the fun and frivolous Circus Egg Cozies (see page 96) and the "Such a Pretty Face" Mirror Case (see page 28).

My dad has a box at home that holds many of the little presents my sister and I have made him over the years. When I told him I was working on this book he went and dug out some of my early felt creations for "inspiration." Although I haven't given you a pattern for the tiny felt computer and monitor I made for him when I was about 8, I have reinterpreted several techniques and projects that I learned at Playgroup, Brownies, and, of course, from my parents. The Geometric Mat (see page 90) was inspired by bookmarks I used to make from old Christmas cards, and paper versions of the Heart Baskets (see page 62) were Easter staples in our house. I was also influenced by my travels to Japan and Finland, as the simplicity and quirkiness of their native crafts are perfect for interpreting in the medium of felt. The Darling Dollies (see page 48) were created from a doodle I drew while watching old musicals (my favorite thing to have on while I am working.) And a walk in the forest near my parents' house inspired my Autumn Garland (see page 72). You can take inspiration from anywhere.

What is so wonderful about felt is that it is easy to work with, it doesn't fray or stretch, and there isn't a right or wrong side. As a novice sewer you really can't go that wrong with it. You can create all the projects in this book regardless of whether you have a sewing machine, as they can all be hand sewn or machine stitched, with both methods achieving beautiful results. Some even require no sewing at all!

I have loved making this book—it has been a pleasure to have a real reason to just sit down and sew. To be able to take my little doodles and make them into wonderful, three-dimensional characters and objects is a joy. I really hope that you enjoy making these projects as much as I have and are even inspired to start creating some of your very own.

Christine x

EXTRA!

If you are looking for more inspiration try my blog:
www.sewyeah.co.uk

HELPFUL!

HOW TO USE THIS BOOK

The projects in this book are either hand or machine stitched (or require no stitching at all!), but, don't worry, if you don't have a sewing machine they can all be stitched by hand (and vice versa). However, you will find that some of the projects are more successful when sewn by hand. For example, the Darling Dollies (see page 48) have very thin arms and legs, which require delicate hand-stitching that will prove much easier to hide, and the shape of the Winged Slippers (see page 24) is slightly too intricate to fit under a machine foot. You can see the difference between hand versus machine stitching on the Pear Doorstop (see page 86) and the Apple Rattle (see page 20). These projects have a similar pattern but are stitched together differently. Essentially, stitching by hand adds a little rustic charm to your projects, while working with a machine achieves a clean, sophisticated finish.

All of the projects in this book are versatile. You can mix and match the makes and their embroidery and decorations, the colors can all be changed, or the scale of the projects can be varied to create a whole new range of items. Enlarge the Woodland Finger Puppets (see page 40) to make them into egg cozies, or stuff and sew closed to make them into cute soft toys. The Circus Egg Cozies (see page 94) can be made into a brilliant mobile using the method for the Elephant Mobile (see page 36) and threading several apples (see page 20) and pears (see page 86) onto a ribbon would make a delightful garland. Re-size the Geometric Mat (see page 90) pattern and make yourself a whole range of place settings and coasters. Or make a giant "Such a Pretty Face" Mirror Case (see page 28) into a pillow cover. The list really is endless.

MATERIALS

WHAT IS FELT?

Felt is a nonwoven fabric that has been around for hundreds of years. Made by heating, matting, and squashing woolen fibers into sheets of cloth, it comes in a variety of weights and it has millions of uses other than for crafting, such as house building (this ranges from insulating roofs to acting as the main construction material of Nomad tents in parts of Asia), musical instruments (the felt helps to dampen the sound of instruments including symbols so that they are not Quite. So. Loud), and in fashion (the felt is heated and shaped into hats and slippers and used to embellish coats and jumpers).

100% ACRYLIC AND ACRYLIC-WOOL FELT

Felt has moved on from the bright, primary colored acrylic ever present in the playgroups and classrooms of my younger days. Though this 100% acrylic felt is still popular (and cheap), I find it difficult to work with as it has a tendency to stretch and loose its shape and it produces a squeaky noise when it is cut that really sets my teeth on edge! However, it does come in a lot of different looks, from leopard-print to glitter, so it is great for making your projects unique.

You can also easily buy felt that is a mix of 60% acrylic and 40% wool. This is nicer to work with than the 100% acrylic and it holds its shape much better. Both of these acrylic felts are usually sold in small or large squares and sometimes by the yard.

100% WOOL FELT

Beautifully soft and strong, 100% wool felt is now widely available and far superior to any acrylic mix. It holds its shape extremely well and comes in an array of colors, from calming neutrals to eye-catching, vibrant colors. Even though it doesn't come printed with different patterns, there is a range of natural marl colors that have a slight fleck, which are great for homewares and stuffed animals.

100% wool felt is available in a variety of different thicknesses, ranging from 1.2 mm to 5 mm, and is sold either in sheets or off the roll—perfect if you are making a larger project. Several online companies (see Resources, page 126) can provide you with swatches of each color, which is really useful for when you are planning your projects. You can also buy 100% wool felt that has been dyed naturally, a process that creates a very soft and muted felt.

I have used 100% wool felt to make the projects in this book. If you can get hold of it, then it really is nicer to work with than the acrylic types and as the majority of the projects are small it won't break the bank!

FELT SHAPES

You can also buy a selection of felt accessories in different shapes, sizes, and colors. From ready-cut flowers and stars to embroidered, beaded balls and ropes, these are perfect for adding decorations and unique designs to each of your projects.

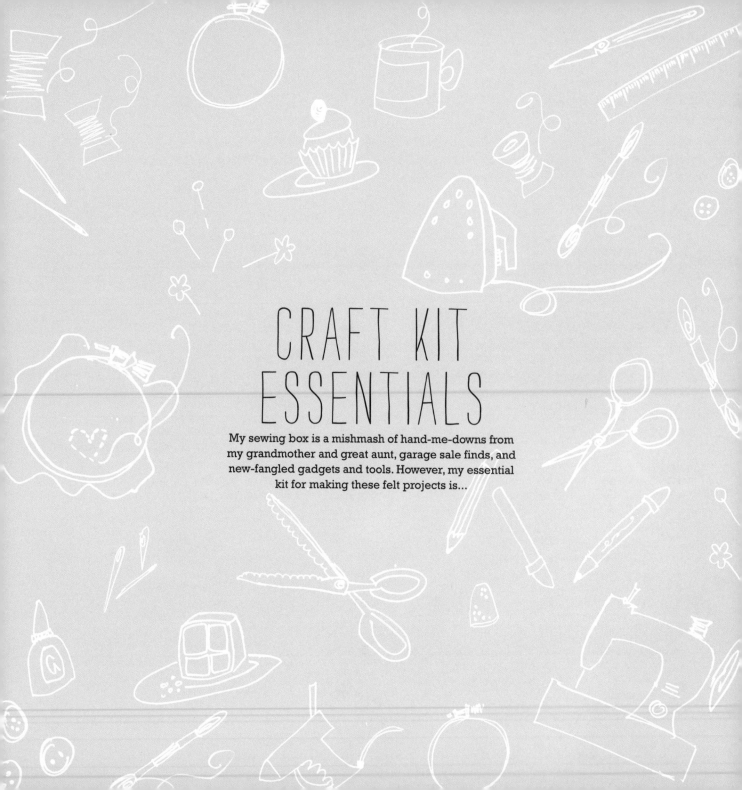

CRAFT KIT ESSENTIALS

My sewing box is a mishmash of hand-me-downs from my grandmother and great aunt, garage sale finds, and new-fangled gadgets and tools. However, my essential kit for making these felt projects is...

SCISSORS

Good-quality fabric scissors are a must as they will easily and neatly cut the felt. Small embroidery scissors are great for snipping threads and for cutting tricky corners or curved edges. I also love to use pinking shears and I have just invested in scallop scissors that give a frilly edge to the bottom of skirts and flowers.

NEEDLES AND PINS

A variety of needles are good to have on hand. Buy a mixed pack of embroidery needles and "sharps" and you'll have a good selection to choose from.

* Thin needles with small eyes are useful for hand sewing ears and accessories to your projects. For example, use them on the ears of the Elephants (see page 36), the flowers on the Heart Baskets (see page 62) and to fix the flaps on the Geometric Mat (see page 90).

* Embroidery needles and embroidery floss are useful for hand stitching and embroidery. A long needle with a big eye or a darning needle can be useful for threading ribbon through the middle of the projects like the Hanging Bluebirds (see page 76) or through stuffing, the Apple Rattle (see page 20).

* A knitting needle or bradawl is good for making holes in felt, but remember to have something soft like a piece of cork or some thick cardboard underneath your felt so that you don't ruin any furniture.

* Use flat-headed pins to pin the felt together before you start to stitch as they are easy to spot and safely go under the foot of a sewing machine.

* Always pin across your line of stitches and never in the same direction.

THREADS

Embroidery floss comes in an array of colors. They can either match the felt perfectly or contrast with it. All the hand-sewn projects use embroidery floss apart from the Darling Dollies (see page 48), which are hand sewn together with sewing thread. A skein of embroidery floss is made up of six thin strands loosely twisted together, which are easy to separate and use individually. The projects in the book use four strands for the main sewing and two for the more detailed embroidery.

GLUES

Fabric glue is good for fixing two pieces of felt together when the stitching would be too visible or for a speedy way of fixing sequins or feathers in place. Follow the manufacturer's instructions to get the perfect bond.

Using a hot glue gun is a quick way of attaching felt to different materials, for example fixing the flowers to the wooden wreath (see page 58). Solid glue sticks are melted in the gun and you squeeze the trigger to distribute the glue where you want it. These are relatively cheap and amazing fun to use! But beware: the glue does get hot, so mind your fingers.

The most invaluable product has to be fusible adhesive web. This is an incredibly useful sheet of adhesive that melts when it is ironed. It will bind different fabrics together and prevents fabric from fraying once cut. Many of the projects use two pieces of felt back to back and applying a layer of fusible web between them creates a nice flat, stiff surface to sew, and a really neat edge when cutting out. It also saves on sewing. Follow the manufacturer's instructions for the best results when using fusible web.

OTHER THINGS

There are just a few other odds and ends that I can't quite live without…

* A craft knife or rotary cutter, a metal ruler, a drafting triangle, and a cutting mat will make cutting straight edges and squares much easier.

* An air-erasable pen is brilliant for marking your measurements and drawing shapes.

* Finally, I find that a constant supply of lemon and ginger tea and a couple of flapjacks are always great to have on hand when you are crafting!

How to ...
EMBROIDER SIMPLE STITCHES

There are a few projects within this book that use a variety of embroidery stitches. The Darling Dollies (see page 48) are sewn together using a blanket stitch and Grace has a lovely embroidered skirt.

Lady Rabbit, Miss Squirrel, and Mr. Fox Finger Puppets (see page 42) have embroidered tummies and the elephants on the Elephant Mobile (see page 36) have elaborately embroidered headdresses and saddles.

HOW TO TRANSFER A TEMPLATE

Photocopy the necessary templates from pages 114–125 onto some sheets of paper. As many of the templates overlap, you may need to make multiple copies. Cut out all the shapes. Using an air-erasable pen, draw around the templates directly onto the fabric. Cut out.

TO START SEWING WITHOUT A KNOT

★ Cut a piece of thread twice the length that you will need. Split the thread so that you end up with half the number of strands needed for the project. For example, if a project recommends using six strands of floss, split your floss in half so that you have three strands. Set any extra strands aside for later use.

★ Fold the strands in half and thread the raw ends through the eye of a needle. You should now have a floss of six strands, with a loop at one end.

★ Push your needle into the felt and draw the thread through until only the small loop is left on the reverse (1).

★ Come back through the felt using a very small stitch and thread your needle through the middle of the loop (2).

★ Pull until the loop is flat against the felt. This secures the thread without messy knots. Begin to sew.

RUNNING STITCH

★ Changing the length of your running stitch can create a variety of effects.

★ Even stitches with equal breaks give a regulated, neat finish (1). For a more decorative line, try alternating a long stitch with a short (2), or short stitches with long breaks. Mix two colors by sewing one line of running stitch in one color then going back and filling the gaps with another (3).

THREADED RUNNING STITCH

★ This is a lovely effect. Sew a line of ordinary running stitch. Using a different color, thread the second length of embroidery floss through all the stitches from alternate sides. Do not stitch the second color through the felt at any point, just weave the thread underneath the top of the original stitches (4).

BACKSTITCH (TOP)

★ This is a useful stitch when outlining designs as it creates a solid-looking line.

★ To start, sew a straight stitch and bring the needle up through the back of the felt (1). Then push the needle through at the end of the previous stitch (2).

★ Push your needle back up past the front of the last stitch (3) and bring the needle down at the end of the previous stitch (1). Continue this method by bringing the needle up at 4 and down at 3. Repeat.

ZIGZAG STITCH (BOTTOM)

★ To start, bring your needle out at A. Then make a straight stitch, inserting the needle at B and coming out at C. Complete the stitch by inserting the needle at A and coming out at D ready to start the next stitch. Repeat.

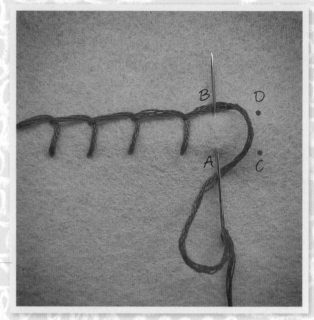

SPLIT STITCH

* Split stitch gives a more delicate finish than a normal running stitch. It looks intricate, but it is actually very quick and simple to do.

* Sew a small straight stitch.

* Take a small backward stitch under the felt and bring the needle back through the center of the previous stitch. This will split the floss into two (1). Repeat.

BLANKET STITCH

* This stitch is good for adding a decorative edge to your felt as well as being useful for joining two pieces of felt together.

* Bring the needle up through the felt where the top edge of the blanket stitch will lie.

* Bring the needle down through the felt at point A and up through point B, threading the needle over the top piece of thread at point B to trap it.

* Push your needle back through the fabric at point C and repeat the previous step, bringing the needle up at point D and trapping the thread at the top.

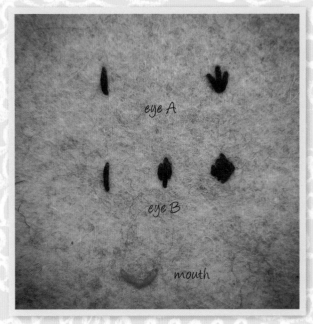

FRENCH KNOTS

* French knots are useful for making eyes, dots, and filling large areas, including the center of flowers. The also give a nice texture to the embroidery.

* Bring the needle up through the felt. Make a tiny stitch through the felt next to the length of floss and wrap the floss around the needle twice (1).

* Push the needle back through the felt, close to the original stitch. The looped floss will slip down and off the needle to create a knot effect (2).

EYES & MOUTHS

* If you don't want to use French knots for eyes, then use one of the options below.

EYE A

* Sew a small straight vertical stitch. Sew a shorter straight stitch at a slight angle that meets with the base of the original stitch. Repeat with another shorter, angled stitch on the other side.

EYE B

* Sew a small straight vertical stitch. This will form the center of the eye. Sew one shorter stitch at each side of the first to create an oval shape. Add one even shorter stitch at each side of those.

MOUTH

* Sew a straight horizontal stitch. Bring your needle up slightly below the middle of the straight stitch. Sew a small stitch slightly lower and over the top of the first stitch, pulling it down into a smile shape (1).

GIFTS

* Apple Rattle * Winged Slippers
* "Such a Pretty Face" Mirror Case
* Cacophony of Clowns * Elephant Mobile
* Woodland Finger Puppets * Darling Dollies

APPLE RATTLE

Apples are good for you, right? Well, although these felt apples will undoubtedly put a smile on your face, I don't recommend you try eating them!

TO MAKE THE RATTLE

1 Using the template from page 115, cut three apple panels from the pink felt and three from the red. Pair up one side of a red panel with a pink and, using pink floss and blanket stitch, stitch together along one long side. Repeat with the remaining panels, alternating the colors, until you only have the first and last panels left to join up.

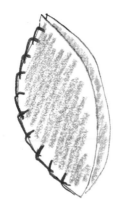

2 Start stitching the first and last panels together, but stop sewing halfway up the apple. Fill with stuffing. If you are making a rattle, push the bell into the center and surround with more stuffing. Finish sewing up the side. If you can see stuffing at the top and bottom of the apple, sew any holes together.

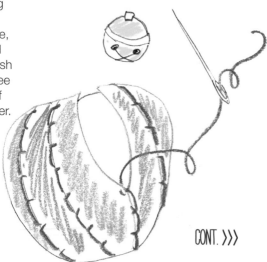

CONT. >>>

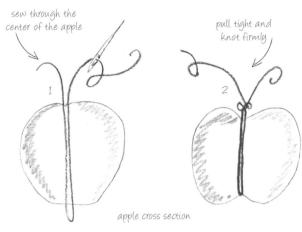

sew through the
center of the apple

pull tight and
knot firmly

1

2

apple cross section

3 To create the apple shape, sew a long stitch through the center from the top to the bottom a few times (1). Pull tight and secure with a knot (2). This pulls the top and bottom of the rattle closer together, giving you the typical apple shape.

4 To make the stalk, fold the brown felt in half lengthwise and stitch around the edges using a running stitch in brown floss.

5 To make the leaf, use fusible adhesive web to fix the patterned fabric to the green felt. Transfer the leaf template on page 115 onto the fabric using the air-erasable pen. With a running stitch in green floss, sew along the edge of the line. Using pinking shears, cut about ¼" outside of the stitching.

6 Sew the bottom of the leaf to the base of the stalk using brown floss, so the leaf wraps around one side of the upright stalk. Firmly sew the stalk to the top of the apple and fold down the leaf.

EXTRA!

These apples are really versatile—by adjusting the size you can make anything from a giant doorstop (see page 86 for the pear example) to tiny apples suitable for a toy grocery.

If you don't want to use a bell you could use a teddy bear squeaker or even some crinkly cellophane to make different noises.

Or make three apples and stuff each one—half with toy stuffing and half with rice—and use as juggling balls.

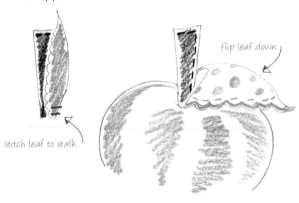

flip leaf down

stitch leaf to stalk

making the stalk and leaf

WINGED SLIPPERS

Hermes was the Olympian God of (amongst others) persuasion, travel, and cunning. His winged boots helped him cover great distances at speed and, hopefully, these slippers will do the same for your divine little being.

The template provided on page 114 is approximately for children's size 2–3. Resize the template for a larger or smaller slipper.

TO MAKE THE SLIPPERS

1 Using the template on page 114, cut out two slipper bodies and two slipper soles from the thick white felt. You will also need to cut out two large stars and four small stars from the yellow felt.

2 Hand sew a large star to the bottom of the soles, using small running stitches in white thread.

3 Line up one short end of the slipper body (A) with the middle of the back of the sole (B). Using a blanket stitch in white thread, sew the sole and upper together. Start by sewing all they way around the sole and then complete the slipper shape by sewing up the back to close. Repeat with the other slipper.

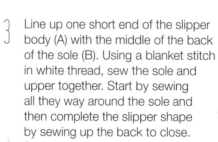

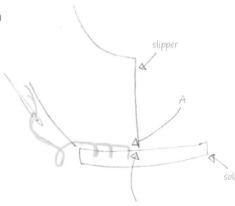

slipper

A

sole

B

CONT. >>>

24

TO MAKE THE WINGS

1 For each wing, cut two 3¼" x 4" rectangles from the thin white felt. Pin together. Then, using the air-erasable pen, transfer the wings from the template on page 114 onto the felt. Stitch around the edge using gold thread. Sew one way and then turn back and repeat for a continuous line.

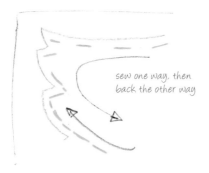

sew one way, then back the other way

2 Carefully embroider the wing pattern using a running stitch and four strands of gold thread.

piece of felt

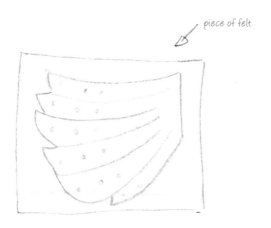

3 Stitch a pattern of white and gold stars (stitch out from a middle point five times, always returning to the central point), and add some white French knots in the gaps between the gold wing lines. When you are happy with the decoration, cut out the shape, about ¼" outside of the stitching line. Repeat to make three more wings.

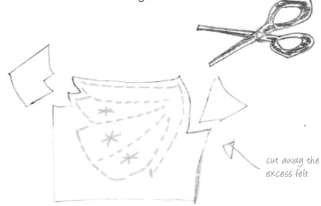

cut away the excess felt

4 Place a small yellow star at the base of each wing, as shown in the photograph on page 25 and, using straight stitches, sew in place against one side of the shoe. Repeat with the remaining wings.

TOP TIP!
Sewing with metallic embroidery thread can be tricky as it tends to snag. If this is the case, use half metallic thread and half embroidery floss in a similar color.

"SUCH A PRETTY FACE" MIRROR CASE

These little cases are great for protecting your mirror and keeping it safe while it is in your bag. It's cute if you make the case in your own likeness.

For each mirror case

Fabric scissors

8" x 8" piece of felt, for head

8" x 8" piece of felt, for hair

Scraps of felt, for cheeks and hair decorations

Iron-on fusible web adhesive

Black and pink embroidery floss

Embroidery thread, in matching colors

Small snap

3¹/₄" circular pocket mirror

makes 1 mirror case

EXTRA!

Enlarge the case and add a long ribbon handle to make a super sweet shoulder bag.

1   Using the templates on page 117, cut out the pieces required. You will need one face, one front hair piece, two back hair pieces, and two cheeks if required.

2   Following the manufacturer's instructions and using fusible adhesive web, stick the two back hair pieces together and stick the face to the front hair. Make sure that the face and front hair form a perfect circle when stuck together. Fuse on the cheeks if using.

3   Following the instructions on page 17, embroider the eyes in black floss and the mouth in pink floss. I have used eye A.

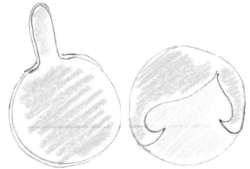

back   front

CONT. >>>

28

HEY PRETTY!

4 Using a thread that matches the hair color, blanket stitch around the top edge from point A to point B on the back hair piece. Repeat on the face piece.

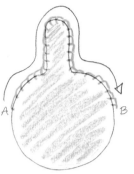

5 Place the face on top of the back hair (with the eyes and mouth outward) so that they line up all the way around and the tab sticks out at the top. Using blanket stitch, sew the face to the back hair from point A to B, but in the opposite direction. This creates a pocket from the lower half of the face for the mirror to sit in. Change the color of the thread to match when sewing the skin or hair.

6 Using thread that matches the hair color, stitch one half of the snap to the bottom of the tab and sew the other half to the corresponding spot on the front hair piece. Place the mirror in the case and check that the snap will close.

7 To disguise the stitching on the tab, use scraps of felt to make a bow, see right. If you like, you could make a feather arrangement or top the bow with a button. Sew in place.

TO MAKE A BOW

1 Using the templates on page 117, cut the pieces out of the felt. Fold the two ends of the main bow (piece 1) in toward the middle and sew in place using a small running stitch. Tightly pull the stitches to gather the bow slightly. Add a couple of extra stitches to the middle to hold in place.

2 Wrap piece 2 around the middle of the bow to cover the stitches. Sew in place at the back. Fold piece 3 in half at a slight angle and sew the fold at the back to create a complete bow.

CACOPHONY OF CLOWNS

I'm not sure what a group of clowns is officially called, but I think the word "cacophony" seems appropriate. When I was younger I made and sold these clowns at the local craft fair.

SUPPLIES

For each clown

Fabric scissors

Scraps of felt in a variety of colors

Bradawl or knitting needle

12" length of pipe cleaner

Fabric glue

4 small wooden beads

Pinking shears

3/4" felt ball

Fabric pens

makes 1

NOTE
Not suitable for small children

1   Cut ⅝" circles from the scraps of felt. You will need 14 circles for the body, 14 for each arm, and 16 for each leg. From each of the body, arm, and leg piles take five circles. Cut these groups of five into circles that are ever decreasing in size, making the smallest circle ⅜" in diameter. Using the bradawl, carefully push a hole through the center of each felt circle.

*tapering circles
(don't worry if they're
not perfect circles!)*

2   Cut a 2½" length of pipe cleaner for the body and two 4" lengths for the arms and legs. Make half a skeleton by twisting the center of the arm around the body, leaving a ⅜" gap for the neck at the top.

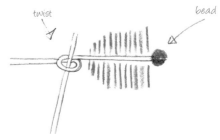

twist   *bead*

3   Thread the arm circles onto each arm. Start with the smallest and add the rest in ascending size. Fold over the ends of the pipe cleaner a few times to hide the sharp ends and, using glue, fix a small bead over each end for hands.

CONT. >>>

4 Thread the circles onto the body. Thread two ⁵⁄₈" circles onto the neck, above the arms. Thread the rest below the arms, starting with the smallest circles. Twist the middle of the leg pipe cleaner around the body pipe cleaner, at the bottom of the circles. Trim any excess pipe cleaner from the body pipe cleaner. Thread the leg circles onto each leg, starting with the smallest circle and adding the remaining in ascending order. Finish with beads for the feet.

FOR THE DOG
Essentially, the dog is made in the same way as the clowns. The only differences are:
1. You will need to squash the felt ball for the head between your hands to make the face an oval.
2. You will need to make felt ears instead of hair.
3. You will need to add an extra 1¼" of pipe cleaner at the end of his body to make into a tail. Finish the tail with a bead.

ta-dah!

5 Using pinking shears, cut a 1½" circle from a scrap of felt for the ruff. Make a hole in the center with the bradawl. Carefully make a hole through one side of the felt ball using the bradawl. Thread the ruff onto the neck pipe cleaner and then push the pipe cleaner into the head hole. Fix in place using a little fabric glue.

6 To make the clown hat, cut a 2"-diameter semicircle from a scrap of felt. Overlap one of the sides to create a cone shape and glue the long straight sides together. Cut a 1½" circle for the hair and make small incisions all the way around the outside edge—do not cut all the way through.

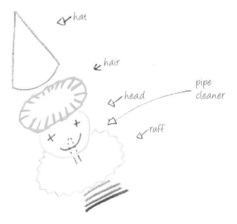

hat
hair
head
pipe cleaner
ruff

7 Using fabric glue, stick the hair toward the back of the top of the head and attach the hat on top. Use fabric pens to draw a face onto the front of the felt ball. Cut small floral or button shapes for the front of the clown's outfit and stick in place using some fabric glue.

ELEPHANT MOBILE

Like the pretty dancing elephants in Walt Disney's *Fantasia*, these decorated elephants will have you all in a spin.

Fabric scissors

Air-erasable pen

Appliqué glue

6¹/₄" embroidery hoop

1¹/₄ yd of pompom trim

For each of the four elephants

8¹/₄" x 11¹/₂" piece of thin felt

Sewing thread, in matching
  colors

Embroidery thread,
  in contrasting colors

Sequins and beads

Small feather

makes 1 mobile

TO MAKE THE ELEPHANTS

1 Cut the piece of felt in half widthwise. Using an air-erasable pen, draw around the body template on page 115 onto one half of the felt. Place this piece of felt on top of the other and pin together. Machine stitch all the way around the pen line, using a medium length straight stitch in a matching color. Cut around the outside of the elephant shape, about ¹/₄" from the stitching line.

2 Choose an embroidery pattern from page 39 and draw the headdress and blanket onto the elephant using an air-erasable pen. Using the stitch guide (see page 39), add some decorative embroidery to the elephant. When you are using running and straight stitches, keep an eye on your needle as you will be stitching both sides at the same time.

3 Using appliqué glue, add sequins to both sides of each elephant where shown. Embroider the eyes using five straight stitches—one long stitch in the middle with two shorter stitches on each side (see page 17).

4 Add glue to the feather end and position between the layers of felt at point A of the elephants head. If it is difficult to slide in, make the hole between the stitches larger by gently pushing a large needle between the layers of felt.

CONT. >>>

〉〉〉

5 Following the template on page 115, cut out the ears. Sew one to each side of the body, using a small running stitch in a matching thread.

6 Cut three 32" lengths of embroidery thread in contrasting colors. Stitch the first through the stitching at point B on elephant's back and knot in place. Repeat with the other pieces of thread. Braid the three lengths together. You want the braid to be as tight as possible and about 12" in length. Once complete, tie off the end. Thread on a couple of beads to disguise the stitches at the top of the elephant.

7 Repeat steps 1–6 to make three more elephants.

TO MAKE THE MOBILE

1 Remove the outer ring of the embroidery hoop. Tie each braid around the inner hoop, placing an elephant at each quarter point. Either hang them all so that they are about 6" from the hoop or vary the distances, making sure that you leave enough of the top of the braids to tie all the ends together.

2 Tie all four ends of the braids together at the top, then tie a second knot ³/₄" below the first to form a loop.

3 Place the outer ring of the hoop back over the inner, covering the knots. Glue a length of the pompom trim around the hoop to decorate it.

4 Use the loop of braids to hang the mobile from the ceiling and watch the elephants dance!

EXTRA!

Make a vertical mobile by following the instructions for the Hanging Bluebirds on page 76, just replace the bluebirds with the elephants.

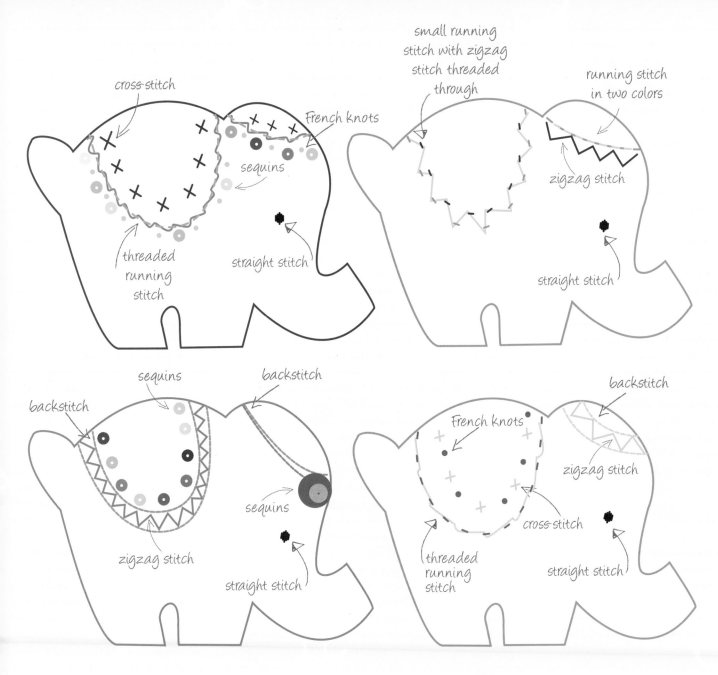

cross-stitch

small running stitch with zigzag stitch threaded through

running stitch in two colors

French knots

sequins

zigzag stitch

threaded running stitch

straight stitch

straight stitch

sequins

backstitch

backstitch

backstitch

French knots

zigzag stitch

sequins

cross-stitch

zigzag stitch

straight stitch

threaded running stitch

straight stitch

FOR STITCHES SEE P.14-17

WOODLAND FINGER PUPPETS

Say hello to my friends of the forest. I think that Miss Squirrel has to be my favorite—I love the way it looks like she is wearing a superhero mask!

SUPPLIES

For Lady Rabbit

4" x 4" pieces of white, pink, light gray, and dark gray felt

Embroidery floss, in matching colors and black

3/8" white pompom

For Mr. Fox

4" x 4" pieces of brown, white, dark orange, and bright orange felt

Embroidery floss, in matching colors and black

For Miss Squirrel

4" x 4" pieces of white, light gray marl, and dark gray marl felt

Embroidery floss, in matching colors and black and beige

For Lord Owl

4" x 4" pieces of light brown, yellow, green, and dark brown felt

Embroidery floss, in matching colors and dark green

All the finger puppets are made in a similar way. I have given detailed instructions for Lady Rabbit and then variations for her friends.

TO MAKE LADY RABBIT

1 Cut out all the rabbit pieces from the templates provided on page 116. You will need two light gray heads, two dark gray bodies, two pink inner ears, and one white face.

2 Using a split stitch and two strands of pink embroidery floss, stitch the design on the right on her tummy.

CONT. 〉〉〉

42

LITTLE PUPPETS + FINGERS = LOTS OF FUN!

PUPPET POWER!

3 Embroider two black French knot eyes (see page 17) and a single pink cross-stitch nose onto the white face. Stitch the two pink inner ears to the middle of the ears on one of the head pieces, using little pink stitches. Stitch the face to the same head piece in line with the bottom of the head, using small white stitches.

sew on

4 Sew the front and back of the head together, using small light gray stitches and leaving a ⅝" gap along one side of the neck area. Gently stuff the head using scraps of felt. Sew the hole closed.

stuff then sew

5 Using the same length of thread, push the needle, at an angle, through the stitching at the bottom of the front of the head piece so that the needle reappears at the middle of the back of the head. Continue to use this length of thread to sew the back of the head to the top of the front of the body of the rabbit. Finish securely.

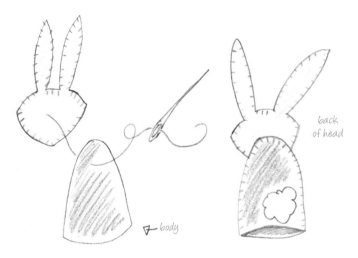

body

back of head

6 Stitch the pompom to the bottom of the back body piece to create a fluffy tail. Using small overcast stitches in dark gray thread, sew the back of the body to the front, leaving the bottom open to create a space for a finger.

CONT. >>>

TO MAKE MR. FOX

1 Cut all the fox pieces from the templates on page 116: one brown head, one brown ear, one dark orange eye, one white muzzle, one bright orange forehead, two bright orange bodies, one dark orange tail, and one white tail tip. Using split stitch and two strands of white floss, stitch the design below on his tummy.

2 For his face, lay the eyes and muzzle over the ears and stitch together. Place the forehead at the top of the front of the head between the ears and stitch in place. Embroider his eyes and nose tip in black.

3 Sew the white tail tip to the orange tail. Stitch the front and rear heads together and stuff. Stitch the head to the front body. Sew the tail at an angle to the back of the body using a few running stitches in dark orange thread. Finally, stitch the front and back of the body together, leaving a finger opening at the bottom.

TO MAKE MISS SQUIRREL

1 Cut all the squirrel pieces from the templates on page 116: one light gray head, one light gray face, one white muzzle, two light gray bodies, and one dark gray tail. Using split stitch and two strands of beige floss, stitch the design below on her tummy.

2 Sew the face to the top of the white muzzle. Embroider the eyes. Stitch the front and rear heads together and stuff. Stitch the head to the front body. Sew the tail to the back of the body, using a few running stitches in dark gray thread. Stitch the front and back of the body together, leaving an opening at the bottom for a finger.

TO MAKE LORD OWL

1 Cut all the owl pieces from the templates on page 117: two dark brown heads, one light brown beak, two yellow eyes, two dark brown wings, two light brown bodies, one light brown small feather, one yellow medium feather, and one green large feather. Using a long stitch and two strands of yellow floss, stitch out from the middle of both eyes seven times, always returning to the central point. Using two strands of green embroidery thread, add French knots at the center for pupils.

2 Leaving a small gap between the eyes to create a slight overhang at the sides of his face, stitch the eyes to the front head piece. Line up the beak with the top of the front of the head and stitch in place.

3 Starting with the largest feather and starting at the bottom of the front body piece, stitch the overlapping rows of feathers one at a time. Each set of feathers hides the previous set of stitching.

4 Stitch the front and rear heads together and stuff. Sew the head to the front body piece and then the front and back of the body together, leaving the bottom open for a finger.

5 Wrap the wings around the sides and the back of the body and stitch to the back using small stitches.

fox   squirrel

DARLING DOLLIES

I spend a lot of time watching old films while making my projects and these dolls are a homage to the movie stars: feisty Audrey Hepburn in *Funny Face* and graceful Grace Kelly in *High Society*.

Air-erasable pen or tailor's chalk

Fabric scissors

Fabric glue

Pinking shears

For each doll's body
Two 8¼" x 11½" pieces of flesh-toned felt

Flesh-toned sewing thread

Polyester toy stuffing

Black embroidery floss or thread

Pink embroidery floss or thread

3¼" x 3¼" piece of brown or yellow felt

makes 1 doll

TO MAKE AUDREY

1 Using the templates on pages 118–119, cut out two bodies, two legs, and two arms from the flesh-toned felt. Fold an arm in half lengthwise and, using a small blanket stitch in a matching thread, sew along the length of the arm leaving the wider end open. Fill with toy stuffing until quite firm. Repeat with the other arm and the legs.

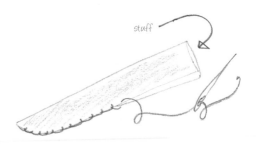

stuff

2 Using short straight stitches in black floss, embroider Audrey's eyes onto her face. Alternate the length of the stitches at the top to give her eyelashes. Use the pink floss to make her mouth—make two close horizontal stitches with one vertical stitch in the middle so that she appears to be smiling (see page 17). For a delicate stitch use only four strands of embroidery floss.

CONT. >>>

3   Following the template on page 118, cut her hair (front and back) out of the brown felt. Place the two body pieces on top of each other and sandwich her head between the front and back hair pieces. Pin together. Using a small blanket stitch sew around her head using brown thread, from one side of her neck around the top of her head to the other side. Using the opening at her neck, fill her head well with some of the toy stuffing.

4   Pin one arm between the front and the rear of the two body pieces. It should be placed at the top of the body and angled so that it slopes down slightly (make sure the arm seam is at the back and can't be seen from the front). Using blanket stitch, start sewing the body seam from the neckline down, working toward the bottom of the body. When you get to the arm use a small stab stitch through the front and back fabric as well as the arm to hold it in place.

5   At the base of the body sew one leg in place (again with the leg seam at the rear) and then the other. Before sewing up the other side of the body, stuff it with toy stuffing, then sew up (but not forgetting to insert the second arm at the top).

front

seam at rear

stuff

CONT. >>>

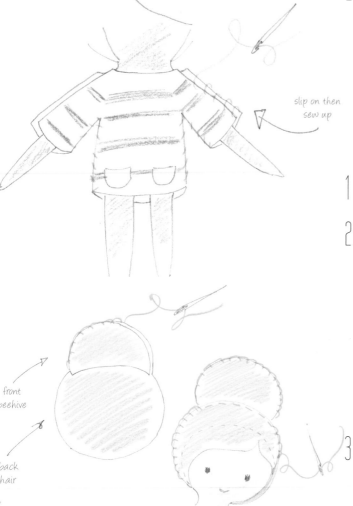

>>>

For Audrey's outfit

$8^1/_4$" x $11^1/_2$" pieces of black and white felt

4" x 4" of blue felt

White and black sewing thread

slip on then
sew up

front
beehive

back
hair

TO MAKE AUDREY'S OUTFIT

1 **For the trousers:** Using the template on page 118, cut out two trouser shapes from black felt and blanket stitch together along the four long sides.

2 **For the top:** Using the templates on page 118, cut out two tops from white felt, and two square pockets if you like. Blanket stitch the tops together along the underarms and body, leaving the top of the arms open. Cut out fourteen $^1/_4$" x $3^1/_2$" strips of blue felt. Glue the strips to the front and back of the top in a horizontal pattern, trimming and shaping them around the arms. Sew the pockets to the top. Slip on the top by working it up over her legs, then sew up the upper arms to hold in place. Put on the trousers.

TO MAKE GRACE

1 Follow steps 1 and 2 on page 48 for Audrey.

2 Using the templates, cut Grace's beehive and bangs from yellow felt. Sew the front of the beehive to the back from point A around the top to B then stuff the pocket. Lay her body pieces on top of the hair and her two bangs pieces on top of this so that they slightly overlap the front of the beehive. Pin together and, using yellow thread, sew her bangs to the beehive starting at C. When you get to A stop and sew across to B, sewing the bangs to the beehive. This will hold her head in place. Continue sewing from B to D. With matching thread, sew the rest of her face to her hair. Stuff her head.

3 Finish Grace by following steps 4 and 5 on page 51 for how to make Audrey.

CONT. >>>

〉〉〉

TO MAKE GRACE'S OUTFIT

1 **For the hair band:** Using pinking shears, cut six
$^{3}/_{8}$" circles from the white felt. Cut a few small leaf
shapes from the green felt. Position on top of the
beehive and stitch in place through the front and the
back of the beehive, pulling the stitches tight to give
the hair shape. If you like, you can add a few pearls
and small beads as you stitch.

2 **For her dress:** Using the template on page 119, cut
out the dress pieces from the light blue felt. Cut the
bottom of her skirt using pinking shears. Embroider
the flower design at the right on the bottom of the
front of the skirt using white and silver floss threaded
with a few silver beads. Cut out small felt flowers
using scallop scissors and stitch a bead in the
middle. Use a little glue to stick on. Using blanket
stitch, sew the skirt pieces together along the two
long sides and gather at the top. Do this by sewing
an even length running stitch around the top leaving
about 4" of thread at each end. Pull these threads
together and gather up the felt to create gentle
pleats. Sew the bottom of the front of the bodice to
the the top of the skirt,
covering up the raw edges
of the felt. Repeat with
the back and sew up the
sides. Slip onto Grace
and sew up the shoulders.
Tie the ribbon sash around
her waist.

3 **For her shoes:** Cut two shoe
pieces from the blue felt and
sew each up the back to form a
shoe shape. Place on her feet and
stitch. Glue on small felt flowers
and beads to decorate.

SUPPLIES

For Grace's outfit
Scraps of white and green felt

Small pearls and beads

Two 8$^{1}/_{4}$" x 11$^{1}/_{2}$" pieces of light
   blue felt

8" of 1$^{1}/_{4}$"-wide white ribbon

White and silver embroidery floss

Light blue sewing thread

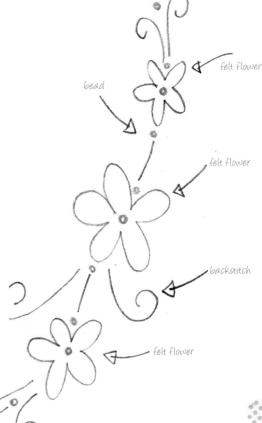

pull

pull

running
stitch

bead

felt flower

felt flower

backstitch

felt flower

DECORATIONS

* Flower Wreath * Heart Baskets
* Bunch of Baubles * Autumn Garland
* Hanging Bluebirds

FLOWER WREATH

This is made up from only three basic flower shapes. They are extremely versatile and using different color combinations and finishes makes each flower look completely different.

EXTRA!

It is the color combinations that make this wreath so versatile. The one shown here is in beautiful spring colors and would be great for an Easter party, but for Christmas try reds, golds, and dark greens. Or pure white and ice blue, sprinkled with a little glitter, or even purple, midnight blue, and copper!

Hang several different-sized wreaths from the ceiling or on a wall to make a lovely display at a wedding.

Once you have mastered making the flowers you will find that they have infinite uses. You could make lovely floral keepsakes in the form of a corsage or a buttonhole.

1 Using the templates on page 115, cut out the desired flower shapes from the different colored felt. To achieve the look in the photograph opposite you will need to cut out about 20 flowers and 10 leaves.

2 Following the step-by-step photographs on pages 60–61, make the flowers. Experiment with combining flower types to create new species. For example, make larger type 3 flowers and use small versions of type 2 flowers for the centers. Sew a few silver beads to the middle of some of the smaller flowers.

3 Decide where you would like the flowers and leaves to go. Add a dot of glue to the back of each with a glue gun and firmly press onto the front of the wreath. Work from one side of your chosen area to the other, keeping the flowers packed close together and adding a few leaves to disguise any gaps.

4 Tie the ribbon around the wreath and hang in your chosen spot.

CONT. >>>

How to ...
MAKE FLOWERS

1 Cut a spiral from a circle of felt...

...roll the spiral up tightly and fix with a little fabric glue.

Use pinking shears for a different effect.

2 Cut leaves from the template on page 115. Use pinking shears and scissor snips for different effects.

...roll the felt tightly...

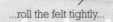

...then fix the end with a little fabric glue.

3 Cut a fronded piece of felt from the template on page 115...

...pull the two threads together to make an open flower or...

...sew a running stitch along the straight edge...

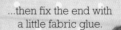

4 Cut a scalloped piece of felt from the template on page 115...

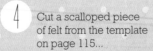

...roll the petals tightly to make a bud.

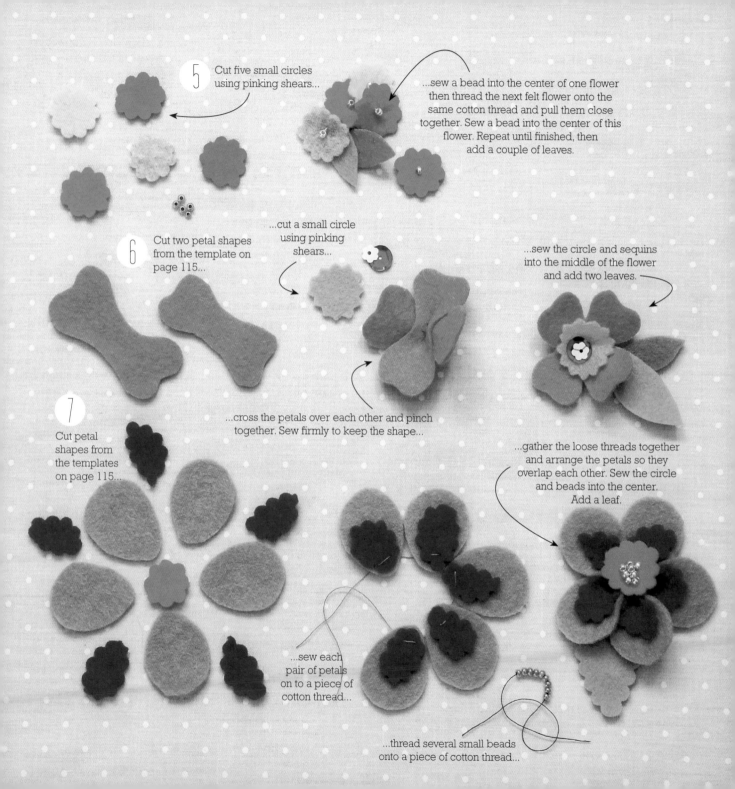

5 Cut five small circles using pinking shears...

...sew a bead into the center of one flower then thread the next felt flower onto the same cotton thread and pull them close together. Sew a bead into the center of this flower. Repeat until finished, then add a couple of leaves.

6 Cut two petal shapes from the template on page 115...

...cut a small circle using pinking shears...

...sew the circle and sequins into the middle of the flower and add two leaves.

...cross the petals over each other and pinch together. Sew firmly to keep the shape...

7 Cut petal shapes from the templates on page 115...

...gather the loose threads together and arrange the petals so they overlap each other. Sew the circle and beads into the center. Add a leaf.

...sew each pair of petals on to a piece of cotton thread...

...thread several small beads onto a piece of cotton thread...

HEART BASKETS

When I was little I made these with my mom's friend, Aunt Jane. We used paper, but felt works really well and is much longer lasting. This is a perfect quick make as it only requires a little glue and stitching!

SUPPLIES

Fabric scissors

For each heart basket

8¼" x 11½" piece of felt in one color

8¼" x 11½" piece of felt in a complementary color

Iron-on fusible adhesive web

Cutting board

Cutting knife

Metal ruler

Sequins and small buttons, for decoration

Fabric glue

makes 1

1 Using the template on page 122 cut out one basket shape from each piece of felt. Following the step-by-step instructions on page 64, weave the rectangles together. When you have finished weaving, press with a damp cloth to help hold the shape.

2 Cut one ¾" x 5½" strip from each piece of felt. Following the manufacturer's instructions, use fusible adhesive web to stick the strips of felt together. If you want a clean edge, trim the rectangles on a cutting board using the cutting knife and ruler.

3 Fold the strip in half widthwise, making a looped handle. Place the handle at the top of the basket, positioning it between the two layers of felt. Stitch each side of the handle to the insides of the basket using small straight stitches.

4 Make some flowers and leaves (see pages 58–61) or add some buttons and sequins to decorate and help to cover the handle stitches. Secure the decorations in place with stitches or fabric glue.

CONT. >>>

How to ...
WEAVE BASKETS

1
Fold both heart pieces in half and begin weaving strip 1. Weave strip 1 through strip c, over strip b and through strip a.

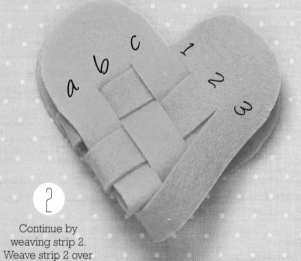

2
Continue by weaving strip 2. Weave strip 2 over strip c, through strip b and over strip a.

3
Finish by weaving strip 3. Weave strip 3 through strip c, over strip b and through strip a.

FILL THE BASKETS WITH
TINY CANDIES, PERFECT FOR
EASTER TREATS

BASKETS OF JOY

BUNCH OF BAUBLES

These baubles are just made from circles of felt. They can be made at any size, just cut all the circles for each bauble at the same size. Tiny ones can be strung together to make a necklace and large ones look great hung above a dining table or a crib.

SUPPLIES

Fabric scissors

For each 4" bauble

Three 8¼" x 11½" pieces of felt

Thread, in matching colors

Thin ribbon or cord, for hanging

Sequins and small beads, for decoration (optional)

makes 1

BAUBLE 1

1 Decide how large you would like your bauble to be and cut out 16 identical circles from your felt.

2 Fold each circle in half and place a damp cloth on top of them. Press with a warm iron to keep folded.

3 Stack all the semi-circles on top of each other and join together with a double length of cotton for strength by sewing through the folded edge of all the circles, once at the top and once at the bottom edge of the folded spines. Leave a 6" length of thread at each end.

4 Tightly pull the two ends of the same piece of thread together and tie with a knot. Repeat with the two other ends of thread, pulling the felt circles together to form a sphere. Thread a piece of ribbon through the center and tie a knot to keep in place.

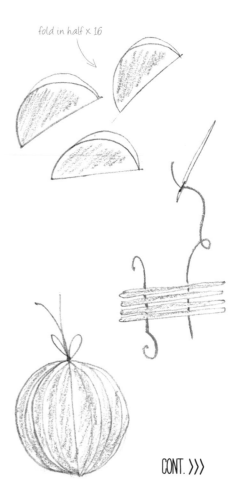

fold in half x 16

CONT. >>>

BAUBLE 2

1 Decide how large you would like your bauble and cut eight identical circles from your chosen felt.

2 Line up and stack all of the circles together and sew a line of running stitch through the center of all the circles to hold in place.

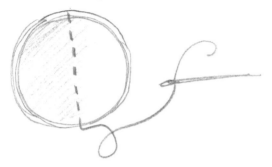

3 Take the top circle and fold it in half along the stitching line. Add a small overcast stitch to the middle of the outside edge of the folded circle (point A) to hold the two together.

4 Turn the stack over and repeat on the other side. Now work around the rest of the leaves, sewing each set of two together as described in step 3.

5 Now you need to stretch the circles into a sphere by sewing alternate leaves together at the top and the bottom (points B and C). This pulls the leaves that have been stitched in the center apart.

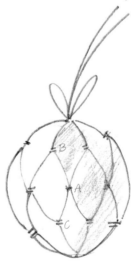

6 Carefully thread a piece of ribbon through the center of the sphere. Tie a knot in one end so that it stays in place.

CONT. 〉〉〉

BAUBLE 3

1 Decide how large you would like your bauble and cut eight identical circles from your chosen felt.

2 Fold each of the circles in half and then half again to create quarters. Add a couple of straight stitches to the pointed end through all layers of felt to ensure the circles remain folded.

fold in quarters

3 Place two of the circles side by side, with the folded straight edges touching. Sew together through the bottom point, using a couple of straight stitches. Repeat with the remaining circles to create four sets of pairs.

4 Sew two of the pairs together, by lining up the two straight edges to make a half sphere of four folded circles. Repeat with the other pairs.

5 Sew the two sets of four together at the folded points, this will help to disguise the stitching in the middle of the sphere. Carefully thread a piece of ribbon through the center of the bauble, making sure it is pulled through the gaps left between the stitching. Tie a knot in one end so that the ribbon stays in place.

VARIATIONS

Use pinking shears to cut out all of the circles.

Decorate the baubles by sewing sequins or small beads at each join or around the edges and thread on smaller felt balls at the top or bottom of your baubles.

THESE BAUBLES MAKE PERFECT
          CHRISTMAS TREE DECORATIONS,
JUST ADD SEQUINS!

AUTUMN GARLAND

To make the templates for this garland, I gathered a variety of leaves while out walking in the woods near my parents' house. I have used oak, horse chestnut, birch, and maple leaves.

Fabric scissors

For the leaves

10–12 pieces of thick felt, in a variety of colors

Sewing threads, in contrasting colors

2"-wide ribbon, at least 2¼" yd long

For the acorns

Scraps of thin brown felt

Pinking shears

Brown sewing thread

Ten 1¼" felt balls, in a variety of colors

Sequins

makes 2¼ yards

TO MAKE THE LEAVES

1 Using the templates on pages 120–121, cut out a mixture of different leaf shapes from the various colors of felt. I find it helps if you lay the leaves out on the floor as you go. This way you can see your shape and pattern forming and see which other leaves you will need to use. For this 2¼-yard-long garland, I made about 30 leaves.

2 A leaf at a time, embroider on the veins using a contrasting color thread. If using a sewing machine, set to freestyle embroidery or a long straight stitch. The sketches (right) show some of the ways that you can sew on the veins. My favorite is one central vein framed by other, smaller ones, branching from the central thread. But you could follow the outline of the leaf, stitch another shape in the center of the leaf or even hand embroider using a selection of decorative stitches such as backstitch, running stitch, and French knots.

CONT. >>>

INSTEAD OF ACORNS
MAKE FLOWERS (P.60)
FOR A SPRINGTIME GARLAND

TO MAKE THE GARLAND

1 Starting 8" in from one end of the ribbon and working toward the other, individually hand sew the leaves onto the ribbon using a running stitch down the center of the ribbon and the leaf. If the leaf falls forward when you hold the garland up, then also stitch along the top edge of the ribbon and through the leaf. Alternate the colors and overlap the leaves to hide any traces of the ribbon.

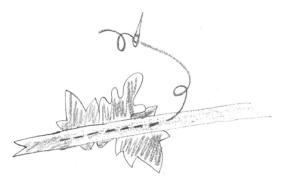

2 Make the acorns according to the instructions on the right. Sew pairs of the acorns at various intervals along the garland's length. Sew through the base of the acorn and the leaf it is being attached to using a long stitch and a double thickness of thread for strength. Repeat a few times to firmly secure the acorns.

3 You can display the garland by either laying it on a book case or over a fireplace (but do beware of any high flames). If you wish the garland to hang down, then use thumbtacks or small nails to secure it in place.

TO MAKE THE ACORNS

1 For each acorn, cut out a $3/4$" x $3^1/4$" rectangle from the brown felt. Cut along one of the long sides using pinking shears to create a decorative edge.

2 Sew the two short sides together to create a closed loop, using small overcast stitches. Using a loose running stitch, sew all the way around one long side and, holding onto one end of the thread, gently pull on the other end. This will gather the felt, creating a cup shape.

3 Take a felt ball and, using a little pressure, roll it between your palms to mold it into an oval shape. Place it in the cup. Sew a single sequin to the top of the acorn, stitching through the center of the sequin and down through center of the acorn, catching in the cup at the bottom. The sequin adds a nice bit of sparkle.

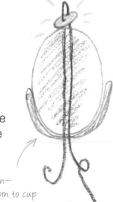

cross section—
sewing acorn to cup

HANGING BLUEBIRDS

The simple shape and stitching of these birds gives a lovely Scandinavian feel to the hanging. This adds a nice decorative edge to a door, but it could also be used as an elaborate light pull.

TO MAKE THE BIRDS

1 For each bird and using template A on page 114, cut out two bird shapes from one of the pieces of blue felt.

2 Transfer template B on page 114 onto the fusible web and cut out. Iron it onto the back of one of the bird shapes following the manufacturer's instructions. Then line up and iron the remaining felt bird to the other side of the fusible web.

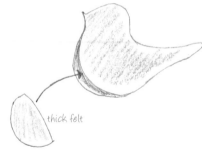

felt

fusible web

3 Using template C on page 114, cut out the tummy padding from the thick felt. Position the thick felt in the cavity left by the absence of fusible web on the bird's tummy. Pin in place.

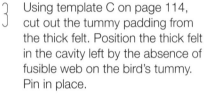

thick felt

4 In a contrasting thread and starting in the middle of his back, use a simple running stitch to neatly sew all the way around the edge of the bird shape. This will hold the stuffing in place and highlight the shape. As the bird will twist in the wind, try to make sure your stitches are neat on both sides.

CONT. 〉〉〉

5 Using the templates on page 114, cut out six wings from the remaining pieces of felt—two small from the second shade, two medium from the third, and two large from the fourth. Layer one of each wing size at an angle, with the largest at the back, and the smallest at the front. Stick them to each other with fabric glue. Repeat with the other wing.

6 Position one wing on each side of the body, covering any unsightly knots, and pin in place. Using two strands of white or dark blue embroidery thread, sew both wings to the body by stitching through all the felt layers at once. I used three straight stitches and a few cross-stitches.

7 Using a single strand of embroidery floss and a small needle, sew a sequin and bead (see right) to each side of the bird's head to create the eyes.

8 Repeat steps 1–7 to make the remaining three birds from the different shades of blue felt.

TO MAKE THE HANGING

1 Tie a bell to one end of the ribbon. Using a large darning needle, thread the ribbon between the stitching at the bottom of one of the birds, up through the middle of the two layers, and out through the top of the bird, between the wings.

2 Using a knitting needle, make two holes in the felt balls and stars by pushing the needle all the way through. Thread a felt ball, a bell, and then another bird onto the ribbon. Repeat this process until you have threaded on the final bird. If your birds, balls, bells, or stars slide down the ribbon when you hold it up, stick in place with a little fabric glue.

3 Thread the remaining felt star onto the ribbon and then thread the ribbon back through the star leaving a loop at the top. Tie a tight knot underneath the star to secure it. Place in a breeze and watch the birds fly.

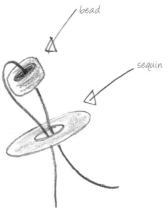

bead

sequin

FOR THE HOME

* Feathered Napkin Rings * Pear Doorstop
* Geometric Mat * Circus Egg Cozies
* Classic Coasters * Windmill Pillow
* Scallop Pillow * Tablet Case

FEATHERED NAPKIN RINGS

This is a simple but effective way to house your napkins and decorate your dinner table.

For each napkin ring

Fabric scissors

Various scraps of colored felt

Matching embroidery thread

Iron-on fusible adhesive web

Fabric glue

makes 1

1 Cut one 1½" x 6¾" rectangle from one felt color and one 1½" x 6" rectangle in a different color. Pin the smaller rectangle to the middle of the larger one, leaving a ³⁄₈" gap at the two ends.

2 Using a running stitch, sew the smaller rectangle in place. With the larger rectangle facing outward, overlap the short sides to form a loop and stitch closed.

3 Using the templates on page 122 and the instructions on page 84, make one small and one large feather for each napkin ring.

4 Place fabric glue along the spine of the large feather and stick it to the front of the ring. Add some glue to the back of the smaller feather and place it at a slight angle on top of the larger one.

CONT. >>>

How to ...
MAKE FEATHERS

1

Using the templates on page 122, cut out the feathers from the felts.

2

Following the lines shown on the template, carefully make diagonal cuts in both sides of the feathers, making sure you don't cut down too far.

3

Slightly stretch the felt by gently pulling on the top and the bottom of the feather. This will open up the individual feather fronds. Carefully snip a tiny piece off each feather frond to give them a curved edge.

4

Wet the felt slightly with a spray of water and fold in half lengthwise. Press with an iron and curl slightly around your fingers.

FEATHERED FRIENDS

PEAR DOORSTOP

This pear is made using the same method as the apples on page 20. Although using a sewing machine gives a neater shape, you can also sew it by hand—just make sure your stitches aren't too big as the beans might fall out!

Fabric scissors

Three 8¼" x 11½" pieces of green felt

Two 8¼" x 11½" pieces of olive felt

Green and brown thread

Polyester toy stuffing

Baking beans, rice, or black-eyed peas

2½" x 2½" piece of brown felt

Iron-on fusible adhesive web

Air-erasable pen

Two 4" x 4" piece of patterned fabric

Pinking shears

makes 1 pear doorstop

1 Using the template on page 115, cut three pear panels from the green felt and three from the olive. Line up one side of a green panel with one side of an olive and, using a sewing machine, stitch together leaving a ¼" seam allowance. Repeat with the remaining panels, alternating the colors, until you only have the first and last panels left to join.

2 Stitch the first and last panels together from the skinny top of the pear downward. Stop sewing halfway down the pear. Turn inside out so that the rough seams are hidden. Fill with a little stuffing. To weigh down the base of the pear, fill a small plastic bag with baking beans, wrap in some stuffing and place inside the pear. Top with more stuffing until firm and hand stitch the opening closed.

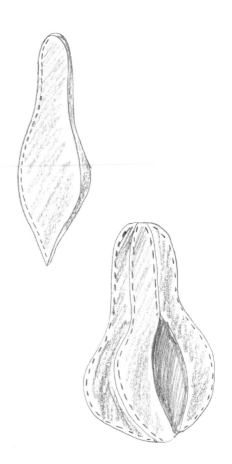

CONT. >>>

MAKE SMALLER PEARS
TO GO WITH
THE APPLES ON P20

NICE PEAR!

3 Fold the brown felt in half lengthwise. Machine stitch along the open sides at a slight angle. Trim away the excess felt.

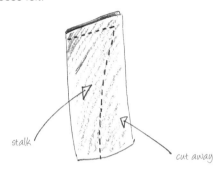

stalk

cut away

4 Use fusible adhesive web to fix the scraps of patterned fabric to the remaining green felt. Use an air-erasable pen and the template on page 115 to draw a leaf outline on each piece of patterned fabric. Machine stitch along the template line. Use the pinking shears to cut around the leaf shapes about 1/4" outside this line.

5 Hand stitch the bottom of the stalk to the top of the pear. Layer the leaves and attach to the base of the stalk with a few stitches and with the felt facing out.

stitches

6 Fold the leaves down to reveal the patterned fabric. Place in front of a suitable door!

GEOMETRIC MAT

I originally learned this pattern at Brownies when making a bookmark out of paper. Felt is a great material to use this pattern on as it cuts easily and doesn't fray. This mat has no specific use, but you could try using it as a coaster, place mat, or plant pot stand.

SUPPLIES

Fabric scissors

Thin paper

Two 8" x 8" pieces of brown felt

7¹/₂" x 7¹/₂" piece of yellow felt

Spray adhesive

Cutting mat

Small metal ruler

Craft knife

1" x 3¹/₄" piece of yellow felt

Yellow sewing thread

makes 1 mat

1 Transfer the template on page 123 onto thin paper. Stick it to one of the two larger brown squares of felt using a fine mist of spray adhesive. Place it on a cutting mat and, carefully following the template lines, use the ruler and craft knife to cut along each line and completely cut out and remove each gray V. Once finished, peel off the template paper.

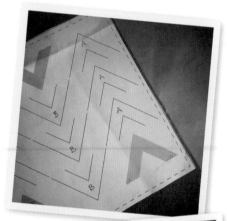

2 Following the annotated template, fold each V marked with an A or B back on itself—the A's should now point downward and the B's should now point upward. Where the points overlap, tuck the A and B pieces underneath the smaller, static triangles (as shown on page 93). Press the folds with a damp cloth to hold.

CONT. 》》

3 Place this piece of cut felt on top of the yellow square, positioning it in the center so that there is an edging of 1/4" of brown felt all the way around. Pin in place at the corners. Stitch a small cross-stitch through both layers at the tip of each V to hold it down.

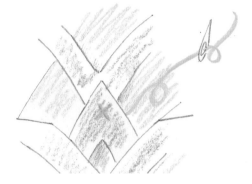

4 Place these two squares on top of the remaining piece of brown felt and pin together. To make the tab, fold the rectangle of yellow felt in half widthwise. Insert the open ends about 5/8" into one corner of the mat, between the layers of felt. Pin. Machine stitch all the layers and the tab together, about 1/4" from the outside edges of the square. Press.

EXTRA!

Once you've mastered the basic pattern it can be used in a variety of ways. Bigger squares make lovely pillow covers to complement the Scallop Pillow (page 106). Or make a set of place mats in red and white felt for your festive Christmas dinner table.

CIRCUS EGG COZIES

Breakfast always seems to be a frantic circus act, so here are egg cozies that will keep your eggs warm while entertaining your little monkeys.

ROLL UP! ROLL UP!

THE EXTRAORDINARY ELSPETH THE ELEPHANT

1. Fold the felt piece in half widthwise and pin together. Using the air-erasable pen, transfer the body template from page 125 onto one corner of the felt, about ³/₄" in from the edge.

2. Machine stitch along the template line, leaving the base open. Cut away any excess felt, about ¹/₈" outside of the stitching line.

3. Transfer two ear shapes onto the patterned fabric, using the template from page 125. Use fusible adhesive web to stick the wrong side of the fabric to a scrap of pink felt.

4. Cut out the ears and then, using small overcast stitches, hand sew the ears to the sides of her head.

5. Embroider the eyes by stitching five horizontal straight stitches into an oval shape (see below) and through both felt layers.

SUPPLIES

Air-erasable pen

Fabric scissors

Iron-on fusible adhesive web

Fabric glue

For Elspeth the Elephant

8¹/₄" x 11¹/₂" piece of pink felt

Gray embroidery floss

4" x 8" piece of patterned fabric

BONGO THE BRILLIANT BEAR

SUPPLIES

For Bongo the Bear

8¼" x 11½" piece of brown
marl felt and a lighter brown felt

Dark brown embroidery floss

4" x 4" piece of patterned fabric

1   Fold the darker felt in half widthwise and pin together. Using the air-erasable pen, transfer the body from page 125 onto one corner of the felt, about ¾" in from the edge.

2   Machine stitch along the template line, leaving his neck open. Cut away any excess felt, about ⅛" outside of the stitching line.

3   Repeat steps 1 and 2 to make his head using the lighter felt. Iron fusible adhesive web onto the wrong side of the patterned fabric. Transfer his ear and tummy templates from page 125 onto the fabric and cut out.

4   With the fabric right side out, iron the ears and tummy in place on Bongo. Embroider his eyes by following step 5 of Elspeth the Elephant.

5   Using large stitches, sew through the front layer of his body and the rear of his head to attach. These stitches won't be seen so they don't have to be too neat.

CONT. >>>

COME ONE, COME ALL!

STANLEY THE STUPENDOUS SEAL

1 Fold the felt in half widthwise and pin together. Using the air-erasable pen, transfer the body template from page 124 onto one corner of the felt, about 3/4" in from the edge.

2 Machine stitch along the line, leaving the underneath of his body open. Cut away any excess felt, about 1/8" outside of the stitching line.

3 Using the template from page 124, transfer two flippers onto the patterned fabric. Use fusible adhesive web to stick the wrong side of the fabric to a scrap of gray felt.

4 Cut out the flippers and then, using small overcast stitches, hand sew one flipper to each side of his body.

5 Embroider his eyes by following step 5 of Elspeth the Elephant.

6 Use a little fabric glue to fix the felt ball to the end of his nose. If the ball is too heavy and causes his head and neck to bend, reinforce his head by stuffing his neck with some scraps of felt.

SUPPLIES

For Stanley the Seal

8 1/4" x 11 1/2" piece of gray felt

Gray embroidery floss

4" x 8" piece of patterned fabric

3/4" pink felt ball

LUSCIOUS LINUS THE LION

SUPPLIES

For Linus the Lion

8¼" x 11½" piece of orange felt

Dark brown embroidery floss

6" x 6" piece of patterned fabric

8¼" x 11½" piece of yellow felt

1 Fold the orange felt in half widthwise and pin together. Using the air-erasable pen, transfer the body template from page 124 onto one corner of the felt, about ¾" in from the outside edge.

2 Machine stitch along the line, leaving the base open. Cut away any excess felt, about ⅛" outside of the stitching line. Repeat steps 1 and 2 for his orange head.

3 Using fusible adhesive web, iron the wrong side of the patterned fabric to a corner of the yellow felt. Transfer the large mane template on page 124 onto the fabric and cut out.

4 Transfer the small mane template on page 124 onto the remaining plain yellow felt and cut out.

5 Lay the two mane pieces on the top of his body and use a few large stitches to secure together. Try to not sew through both sides of his body. Embroider Linus's eyes by following step 5 of Elspeth the Elephant.

6 Sew his head to the middle of his mane using large stitches. Stitch through the front layer of Linus's mane and body and the rear of his head. This can be tricky so take your time.

CLASSIC COASTERS

These coasters are extremely simple to make, so are great for even the most inexperienced crafter. The felt soaks up drips and the color coding helps to remind you which glass is yours!

SUPPLIES

For six coasters

Fabric scissors

Twelve $4^3/_4$" x $4^3/_4$" pieces of felt, in 6 different colors

Air-erasable pen

Cutting mat

Craft knife

Metal ruler

Contrasting sewing thread

Pinking or scallop shears

makes 6 coasters

EXTRA!
You can personalize these coasters by embroidering initials or names on the top circle of felt before you sew the pieces together.

1 Use the air-erasable pen to draw around the base of the wine glass. Draw $^3/_4$" from the base of the glass all the way around onto one piece of felt.

2 Place the felt on the cutting mat. Find the center of the circle and, using the craft knife and ruler, carefully cut a slit from $^3/_8$" inside one side of the circle line to the other. Do not cut through the line.

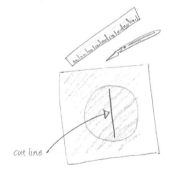

cut line

3 Place this on top of the matching square of colored felt and pin. Stitch around the circle, about $^1/_4$" in from the pen line. If hand sewing, use a simple running stitch or a fancier chain or split stitch.

sew

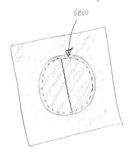

4 Using pinking shears, cut out following the line of the circle. Repeat with the remaining felt.

cut away

WINDMILL PILLOW

~~~~~~~~~~~~~~~~~~~~~~~~~~~~~~~~~~~~~~

**The windmills have a simple geometric feel and are a nice
change from flowers. Choose any color felt to suit your room.**

TO MAKE THE PILLOW COVER

1   For the front panel, cut one 12¹/₂"
x 12¹/₂" felt square. For the back
panels, cut one 12¹/₂" x 9¹/₂"
rectangle and one 12¹/₂" x 5¹/₂".

2   Place the front panel flat on your
work surface. Lay the larger
rectangle in line with one side of
the square and lay the smaller
rectangle in line with the opposite
edge, making sure that all the
outside edges are aligned. The two
back panels should overlap in the
center to make a square the same
size as the front.

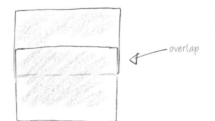

— overlap

3   Pin together the layers of felt.
Using matching thread, stitch
around all four sides about ¹/₄"
in from each edge.

4   Diagonally trim each corner within
¹/₈" of the stitching line. This will
give you neat, sharp corners when
the pillow is turned right side out.

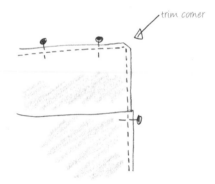

trim corner

5   Turn the pillow cover right side out.
Using the rounded end of a pencil,
gently push the corners out into
neat points. Press.

CONT. >>>

TO MAKE THE WINDMILLS

1 Cut nine 3¼" circles and four 2½" circles from the felt.

2 Make four equally spaced 1¼"-deep cuts into the larger circles and ¾" cuts in the smaller ones. Taking one circle at a time, and in a clockwise motion, fold the edges of each quarter into the center so that they overlap in the middle.

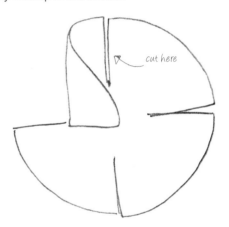

cut here

3 Once all four corners are folded over, secure with a large cross-stitch in a contrasting thread.

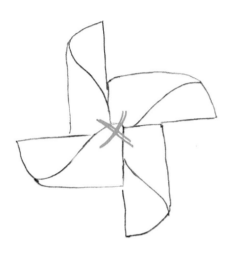

4 Arrange the windmills on the pillow cover front—one large windmill in each corner, one large windmill along each side edge between the corner windmills, and the final large one in the middle. Fill the gaps in between with the small windmills. Stitch the windmills in place by hand using small straight stitches. Try not to sew through the windmills sails.

5 Insert the pillow form into the cover (if you are using a felt that is a nylon and wool blend, be careful not to stretch the felt too much).

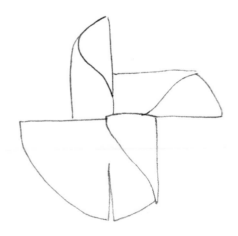

SCALLOP PILLOW

Gray is such a versatile color, it sits comfortably in a neutral color scheme and adds sophistication to a bright one and the scalloped trim adds a more playful edge. Several of these pillows in various colors would look great together.

SUPPLIES

Fabric scissors

1¹/₄ yd x 20" piece of gray marl felt

Matching sewing thread

14" x 14" pillow form

makes 1 pillow

1 Cut one 14¹/₄" x 14¹/₄" felt square for the front panel, two 14¹/₄" x 8³/₄" felt rectangles for the back panels, and sixteen 3¹/₂" felt circles.

2 Place one of the back panels on your work surface and overlap the other back panel on top to create a 14¹/₄" x 14¹/₄" square (it needs to be the same size as the front panel). Baste in place.

3 Starting at one of the corners, pin the circles around the edges of the back panel. Cover each corner with a circle, lining up the center point of the circle with the corner edge of the panel. Along each side and between each corner, pin three more of the circles. Line these up with the corner circles so that half of each circle overlaps with the back cover (see right). Stitch all the way around the outside of the panel, about ¹/₄" in from the outside edge. Remove the basting.

4 Place the back panel on top of the front, with the backs of the circles enclosed between the two felt layers and line up. Sew all the way around the panels, about ¹/₄" in from the outside edge.

5 Remove any remaining pins and carefully insert your pillow form. Take care not to stretch the felt too much while doing this.

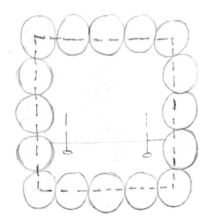

TABLET CASE

Not only does this tablet case protect your precious item, but when opened and rolled back it provides you with a useful angled stand.

SUPPLIES

Fabric scissors

Two 20" x 20" pieces of gray felt

Two 20" x 20" pieces of yellow felt

Large sheet of iron-on fusible adhesive web

Air-erasable pen

Thread, in matching or contrasting colors

Cutting mat

Craft knife

2¹/₂ yd of ³/₄"-wide ribbon

2 large snaps

2 small snaps

2 wooden buttons

makes 1

✳ *The measurements given are for an iPad. See page 112 for how to work out the measurements for other tablet types.*

FOR THE POCKET

1 Cut one 10³/₄" x 8¹/₄" rectangle from each felt color. Place the fusible adhesive web between the felt and follow the manufacturer's instructions to join the layers.

2 With the yellow side up, find the center point by drawing two diagonal lines from corner to corner. The point at which the lines cross is the middle. Use the air-erasable pen to draw a 8" x 6" centered rectangle around this point.

3 Using yellow thread and a small straight stitch, machine stitch the drawn rectangle, about ¹/₈" outside of the line. Stitch along one long side of the rectangle, about ¹/₈" from the edge.

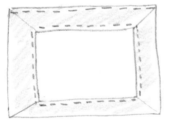

4 Place the felt on the cutting mat and, using the craft knife, cut away the center of the drawn rectangle ¹/₈" in from the stitching line. This will create an open window in the felt rectangle.

CONT. >>>

FOR THE COVER

1 Cut one 10 3/4" x 20" rectangle from each felt color. Cut two 18 1/4" lengths of ribbon. Mark the middle point of the gray rectangle (see step 2, page 108).

2 Pin the two ribbons along the longer sides of the gray felt. Position them 3 1/2" away from the center point and 3/4" in from the edges of both of the shorter sides. Sew the ribbons in place, using a straight stitch in matching thread. Leave a 1 1/4" length of ribbon loose at each end.

3 Use fusible adhesive web to stick the yellow rectangle to the wrong side of the gray felt.

4 Place the rectangle with the ribbon side down on a flat surface, so that the yellow felt is facing upward. Line up the felt pocket with the short bottom edge of the larger rectangle, gray side up, and pin. Using the template on page 122, draw the curved design on the opposite edge of the large rectangle, using the air-erasable pen.

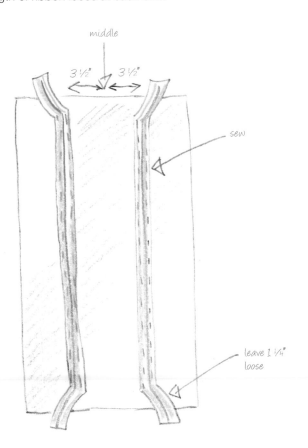

middle

3 1/2"   3 1/2"

sew

leave 1 1/4" loose

5 Using a small straight stitch in yellow thread, machine stitch the outside edge of the rectangle. Starting along one long side of the rectangle, sew around the case ³/₈" in from the outer edge. Sew the pocket to the back panel and around the curve at the top, adding gentle curves to all the corners.

6 Transfer to a cutting mat and, using the craft knife and ruler, trim all the straight sides of the case, about ¹/₄" outside of the stitching line. Use fabric scissors to closely trim around the corners and the curved top. This will create lovely neat edges.

7 Test that your tablet fits in the pocket—if it is too loose, sew another line of stitches along both long sides, just inside the first row.

TO CLOSE THE CASE

1 Fold the ribbons that sit at the curved edge under themselves to hide the raw edges. The ribbon should now be about ³/₈" from the edge of the felt. Trim it if it is too long. Sew a button to the end of the fold to hold it in place. Stitch half a large snap to the underside of the cover, positioned directly beneath the buttons.

OTHER TABLET MEASUREMENTS

POCKET
Width: Add an extra 1¹/₄" to the width of your tablet (Width + 1¹/₄")
Height: Add an extra 1¹/₄" to the height of your tablet (Height + 1¹/₄")

COVER
Width: Add an extra 1¹/₄" to the width of your tablet (Width + 1¹/₄")
Height: Double the height of your tablet and add an extra 5¹/₄" (2 x Height + 5¹/₄")

2 Fold under the raw edges of ribbon at the other end of the case and hand stitch in place using small straight stitches. Place your tablet in the pocket and wrap the cover around it. Mark where the corresponding snap part should sit on the main case and stitch in place.

3 To ensure your tablet is secure in the case, cut two 2¹/₂" lengths of ribbon. Sew half a small snap to one end of each. Fold in half lengthwise and stitch the plain end of ribbon to the inside of the pocket, about 1¹/₂" from the edge. Carefully stitch the other snap part to the inside of the cover, so that the ribbon folds over the top of the tablet. Line it up with the matching ribbon snap.

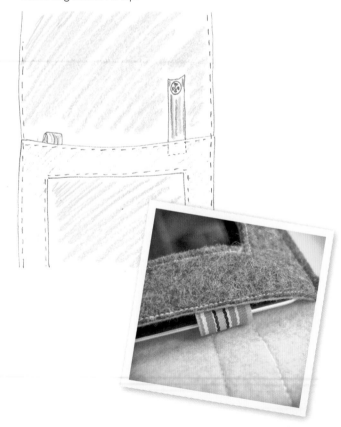

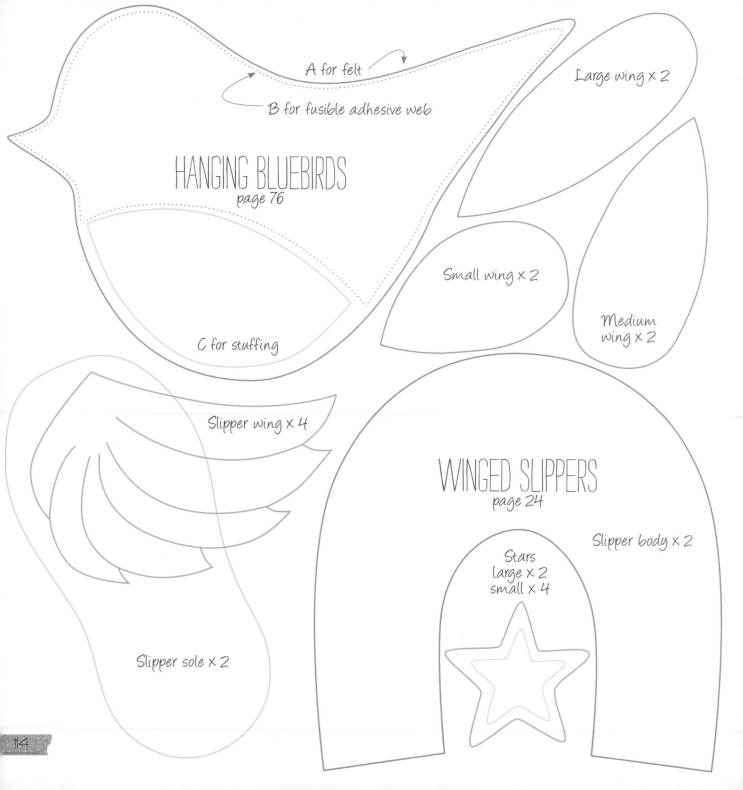

A for felt

B for fusible adhesive web

Large wing x 2

HANGING BLUEBIRDS
page 76

Small wing x 2

Medium wing x 2

C for stuffing

Slipper wing x 4

WINGED SLIPPERS
page 24

Slipper body x 2

Stars
large x 2
small x 4

Slipper sole x 2

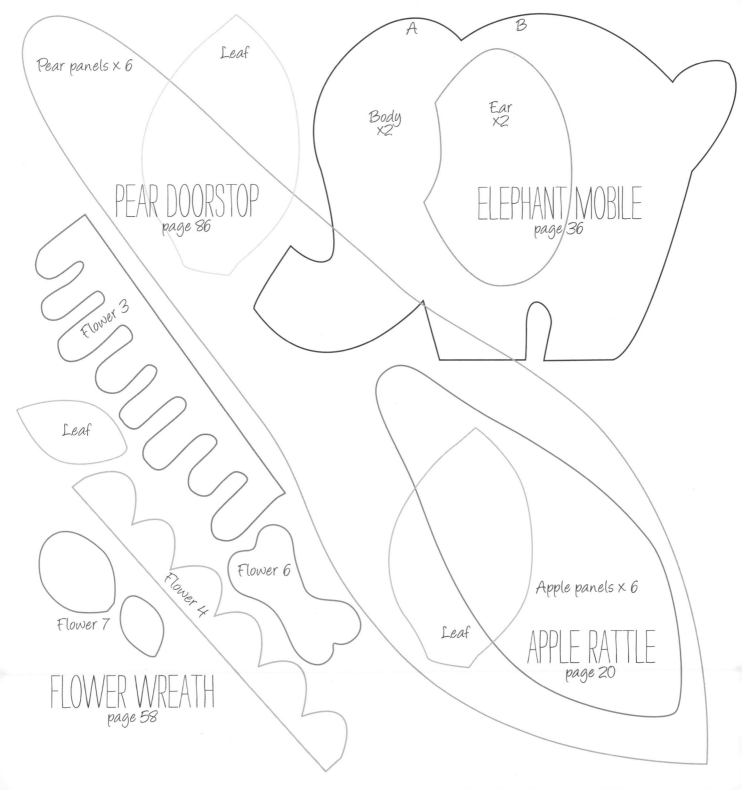

Pear panels × 6

Leaf

PEAR DOORSTOP
page 86

A

B

Body
×2

Ear
×2

ELEPHANT MOBILE
page 36

Flower 3

Leaf

Flower 6

Flower 4

Flower 7

FLOWER WREATH
page 58

Apple panels × 6

Leaf

APPLE RATTLE
page 20

Squirrel head × 1

Squirrel tail × 1

Rabbit face × 1

Rabbit head × 2

Squirrel body × 2

Rabbit body × 2

Squirrel face × 1

Squirrel muzzle × 1

Rabbit inner ears

Fox ears × 1

Fox tail × 1

Fox forehead × 1

Fox head × 1

Fox muzzle × 1

Fox eyes × 1

Fox body × 2

Fox tail tip × 1

WOODLAND FINGER PUPPETS
page 42

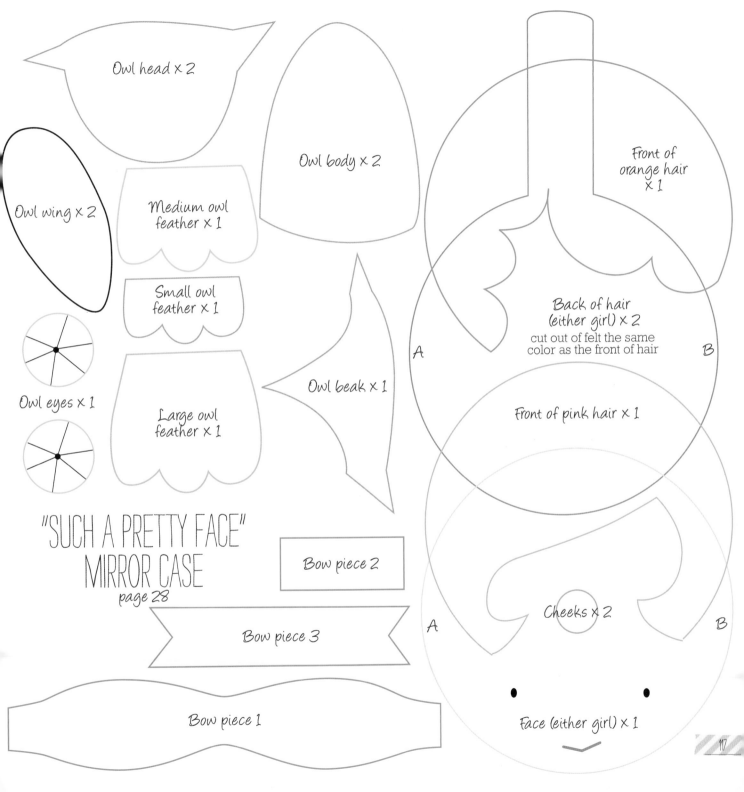

Owl head × 2

Owl body × 2

Front of
orange hair
× 1

Owl wing × 2

Medium owl
feather × 1

Back of hair
(either girl) × 2
cut out of felt the same
color as the front of hair

A

B

Small owl
feather × 1

Owl eyes × 1

Owl beak × 1

Front of pink hair × 1

Large owl
feather × 1

"SUCH A PRETTY FACE"
MIRROR CASE
page 28

Bow piece 2

Cheeks × 2

A

B

Bow piece 3

A

B

Bow piece 1

Face (either girl) × 1

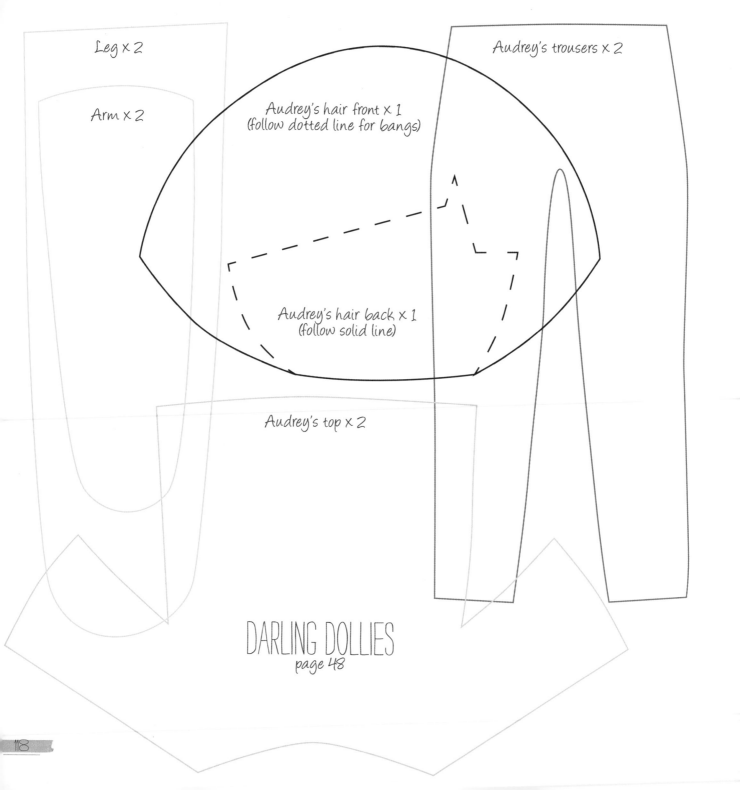

Leg × 2

Arm × 2

Audrey's trousers × 2

Audrey's hair front × 1
(follow dotted line for bangs)

Audrey's hair back × 1
(follow solid line)

Audrey's top × 2

DARLING DOLLIES
page 48

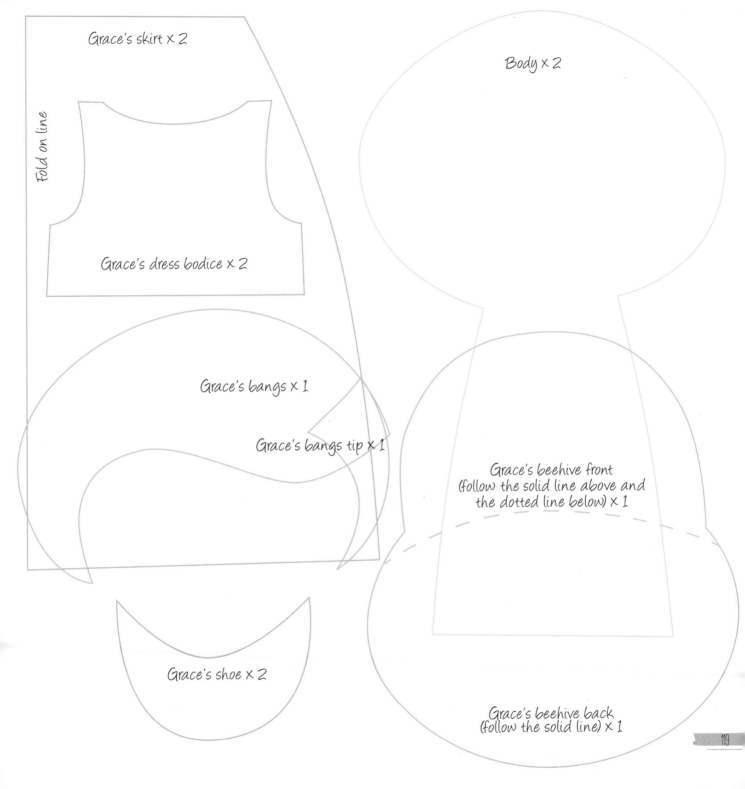

Grace's skirt x 2

Fold on line

Grace's dress bodice x 2

Grace's bangs x 1

Grace's bangs tip x 1

Grace's shoe x 2

Body x 2

Grace's beehive front
(follow the solid line above and
the dotted line below) x 1

Grace's beehive back
(follow the solid line) x 1

AUTUMN GARLAND
page 72

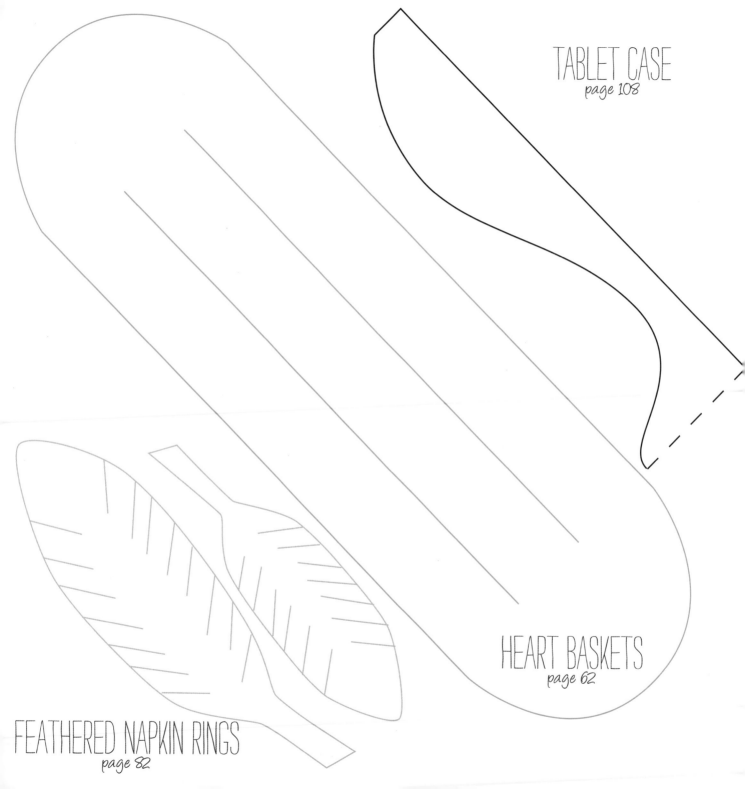

TABLET CASE
page 108

FEATHERED NAPKIN RINGS
page 82

HEART BASKETS
page 62

Stitching line

A

A

A

A

A

A

B

B

B

GEOMETRIC MAT
page 90

Cut gray shaded areas
away completely

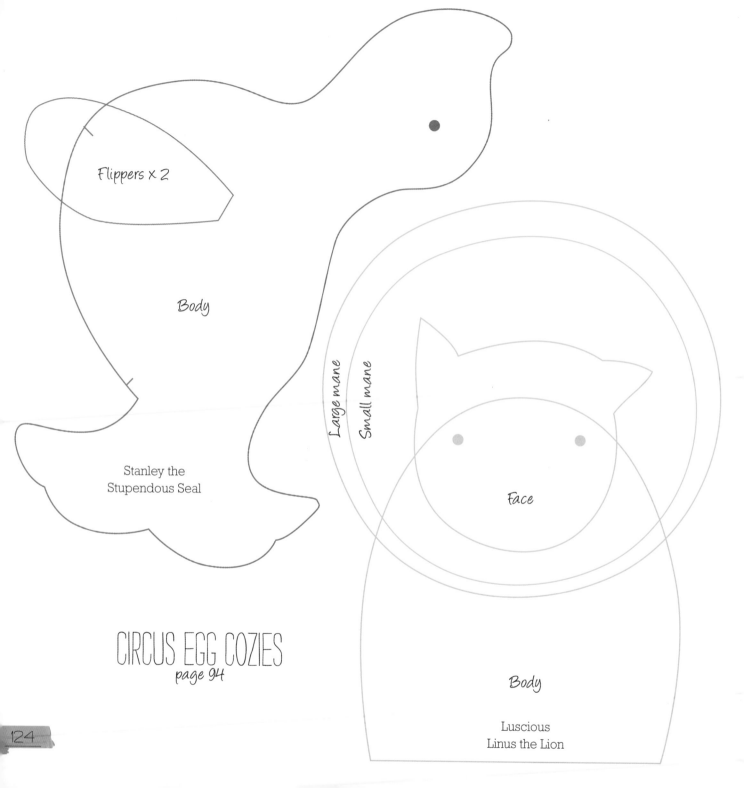

Flippers x 2

Body

Stanley the
Stupendous Seal

Large mane

Small mane

Face

Body

Luscious
Linus the Lion

CIRCUS EGG COZIES
page 94

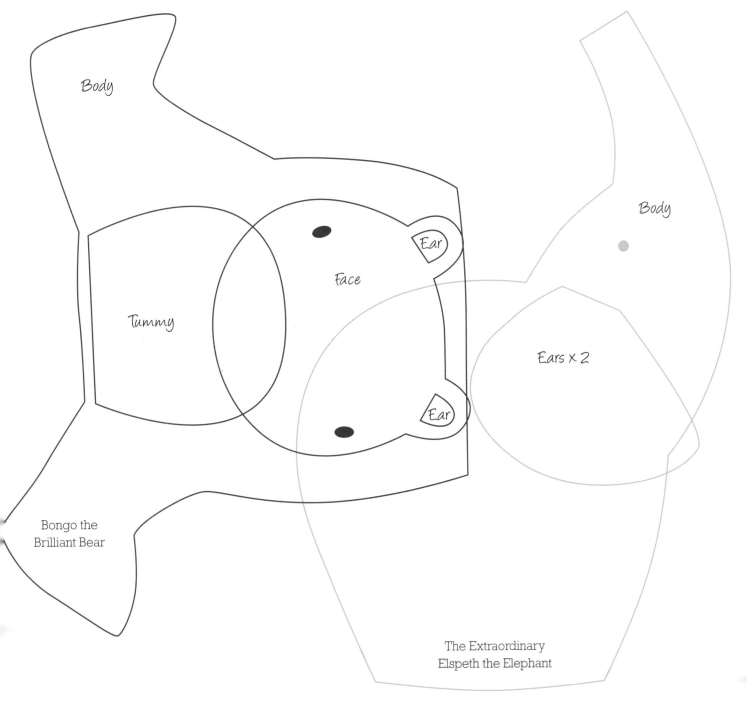

Body

Body

Face

Ear

Ear

Tummy

Ears x 2

Bongo the
Brilliant Bear

The Extraordinary
Elspeth the Elephant

RESOURCES

Here are my favorite sources for felt craft supplies and tools. Find your supplies at your own local craft stores and online sites.

FELT

WOOL FELT COMPANY
Stocks 100% and 30% wool felt in over 70 colors that are sold in squares, by the half meter, or as remnants.
shop@woolfeltcompany.co.uk
www.woolfeltcompany.co.uk

BLOOMING FELT
Sells thick 100% wool felt and 100% woven wool felt that has a weave texture to it. Also stocks a variety of felt shapes.
www.bloomingfelt.co.uk

FELT FOLK
Stocks thick (3–4mm) 100% wool felt in squares and by the metre.
www.feltfolk.com

MYRIAD NATURAL TOYS AND CRAFTS
A great selection of 100% wool felt. They also stock some plant-dyed felt.
www.myriadonline.co.uk

NOTIONS AND FABRIC

BARNETT LAWSON
A wholesaler for lots of trimmings.
16–17 Little Portland Street
London W1W 8NE
www.bltrimmings.com

FABRIC REHAB
Supplies fabrics for patchwork. Stocks cute Japanese designs.
www.fabricrehab.co.uk

ECLECTIC MAKER
Sells many fabulous fabrics and general sewing supplies.
www.eclecticmaker.co.uk

HOBBYCRAFT
A craft superstore.
www.hobbycraft.co.uk

JANE MEANS RIBBONS
An online store that sells a plethora of ribbons.
www.janemeans.com

JO-ANN FABRIC AND CRAFT CENTER
www.joann.com

MICHAEL'S
www.michaels.com

THE STITCHERY
A notions and fabric shop.
www.the-stitchery.co.uk

LIFESTYLE

ANTHROPOLOGIE
Inspiring lifestyle, clothing, and interiors shop.
158 Regent Street,
London W1B 5SW
www.anthropologie.eu

LABOUR AND WAIT
Sells simple, yet beautiful homewares and clothing.
85 Redchurch Street,
London E2 7DJ
www.labourandwait.co.uk

LAURA ASHLEY
A clothing and interiors store. You are guaranteed to pick up a bargain at one of their sales!
www.lauraashley.com

ROCKETT ST GEORGE
A quirky online store selling interior goodies and gifts.
hello@rockettstgeorge.co.uk
www.rockettstgeorge.co.uk

HARLEQUIN WALLPAPERS AND FABRICS
Stocks bold and bright prints in both papers and fabrics.
www.harlequin.uk.com

WHAT ARE YOU LOOKING FOR?

INDEX

THANK YOU THANK YOU THANK YOU

Many thanks must go to Lisa at Quadrille for championing this little book and making it happen. Thanks also to Jane and Helen, and Claire for her design skills and patience. To Louise for reading all the words and making sure they make sense! And to everyone else at Quadrille, they are lovely people to work for.

Big thanks to Stuart and Aelia for letting me take photographs in their beautiful house – hope I didn't make too much mess! Also to lovely Keiko for her amazing photography and calmness, this book is beautiful because of you.

Huge hugs to Jake, Kirsty, and Laura for listening to my ramblings, half-finished sentences and general maniacal behaviour, and to Hannah, because her big ideas and passion got me where I am today.

To all my family – Mum, Dad, Jo, Ian, Oliver and Elliot, Aunty and Uncle, Nanny and Grandad – for their support, belief, encouragement, suggestions, modelling and project testing.

Publishing Director Jane O'Shea
Commissioning Editor Lisa Pendreigh
Editor Louise McKeever
Creative Director Helen Lewis
Art Direction & Design Claire Peters
Designer Katherine Keeble
Photographer Keiko Oikawa
Stylist and Illustrator Christine Leech
Production Director Vincent Smith
Production Controller Aysun Hughes

First edition for the United States and Canada published in 2014
Barron's Educational Series, Inc.

Text, project designs, artwork & illustrations © 2013 Christine Leech
Photography © 2013 Keiko Oikawa
Design & layout © 2013 Quadrille Publishing Ltd

First published in 2013 by
Quadrille Publishing Ltd
www.quadrille.co.uk

All inquiries should be addressed to:
Barron's Educational Series, Inc.
250 Wireless Boulevard
Hauppauge, NY 11788
www.barronseduc.com

ISBN: 978-1-4380-0469-3

Library of Congress Control No.: 2014938261

Printed in China
9 8 7 6 5 4 3 2 1